THE PRINCE

—

# ON THE
# FUTURE
## OF FOOD

—

THE PRINCE'S SPEECH

———

# ON THE
# FUTURE
# OF FOOD

———

HRH THE PRINCE OF WALES

FOREWORD BY
WENDELL BERRY

AFTERWORD BY
WILL ALLEN AND ERIC SCHLOSSER

RODALE.

# CONTENTS

———

THE EXTREME DESTRUCTIVENESS—
AND THEREFORE THE FRAGILITY—OF INDUSTRIAL
AGRICULTURE IS NOT A SECRET.

THE INDUSTRIAL MIND, as it is manifested in agriculture, solves problems one at a time by single solutions usually large in scale and always highly profitable to some branch of agribusiness. Thus to produce the greatest possible quantity of corn in the American Midwest, the approved means is chemical nitrogen in massive doses. This does enable gigantic corn harvests, weather permitting and temporarily, which fulfills the single purpose of nitrogen fertilizer. But to secure this one result it is necessary to ignore vital questions having to do with the health of the soil, of local ecosystems and their watersheds, of the watershed of the Mississippi River, and of the waters of the Gulf of Mexico. Those questions lead in turn to questions about the physical and economic health of human beings. And all those questions lead ultimately, and frighteningly, to questions about the long-term availability of natural gas, from which we make nitrogen fertilizer, with which we grow our present vast acreages of corn.

Vast acreages planted continuously in corn or soybeans produce a lot of corn and soybeans. So many acres, so many bushels per acre, were urgently required, we were told by the publicists and politicians, to "feed the world." Now to that urgent requirement another, equally urgent, has been added: the production of "biofuel" to hasten the day of "energy independence." And so the vast acreages devoted to annual row crops must become yet more vast. As a consequence, all of these millions of acres are annually exposed to erosion and degradation of the soil, and the chemical runoff plays the devil with water quality. Again, we confront the question of long-term sustainability. And the answer is inarguable: This way of food production is destructive of everything it depends on. It can't last.

The extreme destructiveness—and therefore the fragility—of industrial agriculture is not a secret. It is obvious to anybody who will look and learn. Knowledgeable people have been speaking of it and writing about it since the first half of the last century. But those knowledgeable people have been mere citizens. Arrayed against them have been, of course, all agricultural industrialists and all agribusiness corporations, but also all the stars of academic and scientific agriculture and every politician of any significance. It may be understandable that many influential politicians discredit the warnings about climate change, for climate change, maybe, is not obvious. But when practically every economist, scientist, intellectual, and politician ignores or denies agricultural damages that are measurable, massive, and obvious, then we are living just as obviously in an age of official insanity.

So far as I know, only one eminent person has

had both the clarity to see and the courage to speak candidly about the obvious failures and dangers of industrial agriculture. That person is Prince Charles of the United Kingdom, who took his stand and made his challenge to industrial agriculture many years ago. Americans may be inclined to think that he has been free to do this because his position is not elective. But like no American politician, he belongs for life to his constituency, many of whom no doubt expect him to support their conventional assumptions about agriculture. When he speaks of challenging those assumptions as "extremely dangerous" and "a risky business," one may confidently assume that he knows what he is talking about.

In Washington, DC, on May 4, 2011, Prince Charles delivered a speech the text of which is provided in this little book, and which was, by any measure, remarkable. It was most certainly a challenge to conventional assumptions, but it was nothing like the speeches on public issues that we are getting accustomed to in the United States. It was not a volley of angry slogans and loose assertions. On the contrary, Prince Charles's terms were clearly defined; his argument was made carefully and in detail; his speech was quietly voiced, and the more powerful for that. He did not speak as a blinkered partisan of a "side," but rather, as a human to other humans, of concerns urgently important to us all.

He said that we humans are under obligation to increase "the long-term fertility of the soil."

He said that we need "a form of agriculture that does not exceed the carrying capacity of its local ecosystem and which recognizes that the soil is the planet's most vital renewable resource."

He said that we need to do everything possible, and use the best new technology, to conserve water.

He said that "social and economic stability is built upon valuing and supporting local communities and their traditions," and that "smallholder agriculture therefore has a pivotal role."

He said, "Capitalism depends upon capital, but our capital ultimately depends upon the health of Nature's capital."

There is nothing extreme or odd in anything

I have quoted, or in the speech as a whole, which amounts exactly to the good sense that we once recognized as "common." That this sense is now so rarely spoken, and that a prominent man needs rare courage to speak it, tells us how highly we should value this speech, and how fortunate we are to share the world, in our difficult time, with this speaker.

WENDELL BERRY

ON MAY 4, 2011, HIS ROYAL HIGHNESS THE PRINCE OF WALES GAVE THE KEYNOTE SPEECH TO THE FUTURE OF FOOD CONFERENCE AT GEORGETOWN UNIVERSITY, WASHINGTON, DC. THIS ESSAY HAS BEEN ADAPTED FROM THOSE REMARKS.

SOILS ARE BEING DEPLETED, DEMAND FOR
WATER IS GROWING EVER MORE VORACIOUS, AND
THE ENTIRE SYSTEM IS AT THE MERCY OF AN
INCREASINGLY FLUCTUATING PRICE OF OIL.

## THE PRINCE'S SPEECH

THE WORLD is gradually waking up to the fact that creating sustainable food systems will become paramount in the future because of the enormous challenges now facing food production.

The *Oxford English Dictionary* defines "sustainability" as "keeping something going continuously." And the need to "keep things going" for future generations is quite frankly the reason I have been venturing into extremely dangerous territory by speaking about the future of food over the past 30 years. I have all the scars to prove it . . . ! Questioning the conventional worldview is a risky business. And the only reason I have done so is for the sake of the younger generation and for the integrity of Nature herself. It is your future that concerns me and that of your grandchildren, and theirs too. That is how far we should be looking ahead. I have no intention of being confronted by my grandchildren, demanding to know why on Earth we didn't do something about the many problems that existed when we knew what was going wrong. The threat of that question, the responsibility of it, is precisely why I have gone on challenging the assumptions of our day. And I would urge you to do the same, because we need to face up to asking whether how we produce our food is actually fit for purpose in the very challenging circumstances of the 21st century. We simply cannot ignore that question any longer.

Very nearly 30 years ago I began by talking about the issue, but I realized in the end I had to go further. I had to put my concern into action, to demonstrate how else we might do things so that we secure food production for the future, but also, crucially, to take care of the Earth that sustains us. Because if we don't do that, if we do not work within Nature's system, then Nature will fail to be the durable, continuously sustaining force she has always been. Only by safeguarding Nature's resilience can we hope to have a resilient form of food production and ensure food security in the long term.

This is the challenge facing us. We have to maintain a supply of healthy food at affordable prices when there is mounting pressure on nearly every element affecting the process. In some cases we are pushing Nature's life-support systems so far, they are struggling to cope with what we ask of them. Soils are being depleted, demand for water is growing ever more voracious, and the entire system is at the mercy of an increasingly fluctuating price of oil.

Remember that when we talk about agriculture and food production, we are talking about a complex and interrelated system and it is simply not possible to single out just one objective, like maximizing production, without also ensuring that the system which delivers those increased yields meets society's other needs. As Eric Schlosser has highlighted, these should include the maintenance of public health, the safeguarding of rural employment, the protection of the environment, and contributing to overall quality of life.

So we must not shy away from the big questions. Chiefly, how can we create a more sustainable approach to agriculture while recognizing those wider and important social and economic parameters—an approach that is capable of feeding the world with a global population rapidly heading for 9 billion? And can we do so amid so many competing demands on land, in an increasingly volatile climate and when levels of the planet's biodiversity are under such threat or in serious decline?

As I see it, these pressures mean we haven't much choice in the matter. We are going to have to take some very brave steps. We will have to develop much more sustainable or durable forms of food production because the ways we have done things up to now are no longer as viable as they once appeared to be. The more I talk with people about this issue, the more I realize how vague the general picture remains of the perilous state we are in. So, just to be absolutely clear, I offer a quick sketch of just some of the evidence that this is so.

Certainly, internationally, food insecurity is a growing problem. There are also many now who consider that global food systems are well on the way to being in crisis. Yield increases for staple food crops are declining. They have dropped from 3 percent in the 1960s to 1 percent today—and that is really worrying because, for the first time, that rate is less than the rate of population growth. And all of this, of course, has to be set against the ravages caused by climate change. Already yields are suffering in Africa and India, where crops are failing to cope with ever-increasing temperatures and fluctuating rainfall. We all remember the failure of last year's wheat harvest in Russia and droughts in China. They have caused the cost of food to rocket and, with it, inflation around the world, stoking social discontent in many countries, notably in the Middle East. It is a situation I fear will only become more volatile as we suffer yet more natural disasters.

Set against these threats to yields is the ever-growing demand for food. The United Nations

WITH INCOMES RISING IN PLACES LIKE
CHINA AND INDIA, THERE WILL ALSO BE MORE
PEOPLE WEALTHY ENOUGH TO CONSUME
MORE, SO THE DEMAND FOR MEAT AND DAIRY
PRODUCTS MAY WELL INCREASE YET FURTHER.

Food and Agriculture Organization estimates that the demand will rise by 70 percent between now and 2050. The curve is quite astonishing. The world somehow has to find the means of feeding a staggering 219,000 new mouths every day. What is more, with incomes rising in places like China and India, there will also be more people wealthy enough to consume more, so the demand for meat and dairy products may well increase yet further. And all that extra livestock will compete for feed more and more with an energy sector that has massively expanded its demand for biofuels. In the United States, I am told, four out of every ten bushels of corn are now grown to fuel motor vehicles.

This is the context we find ourselves in and it is set against the backdrop of a system heavily dependent upon fossil fuels and other forms of diminishing natural capital—mineral fertilizers and so on. Most forms of industrialized agriculture now have an umbilical dependency on oil, natural gas, and other nonrenewable resources. One study I have read estimates that a person today on a typical Western diet is, in effect, consuming nearly a US gallon of diesel every day! And when you consider that in the past decade the cost of artificial nitrogen fertilizers has gone up fourfold and the cost of potash three times, you start to see how uncomfortable the future could become if we do not wean ourselves off our dependency. And that's not even counting the impact of higher fuel prices on the other costs of production—transportation and processing—all of which are passed on to the consumer. It is indeed a vicious circle.

Then add the supply of land into the equation—where do we grow all of the extra plants or graze all that extra stock when urban expansion is such a pressure? In the United States, I have learned, one acre is lost to development every minute of every day—which means that since 1982 an area the size of Indiana has been built over—though that is small-fry compared with what is happening in places like India where, somehow, they have to find a way of housing another 300 million people in the next 30 years.

And on top of this is the very real problem of

soil erosion. Again, in the United States, soil is being washed away ten times faster than the Earth can replenish it, and it is happening 40 times faster in China and India. Twenty-two thousand square miles of arable land is turning into desert every year and, all told, it appears a quarter of the world's farmland, 2 billion acres, is degraded.

Given these pressures, it seems likely we will have to grow plants in more difficult terrain. But the only sustainable way to do that will be by increasing the long-term fertility of the soil, because, as I say, achieving increased production using imported, nonrenewable inputs is simply not sustainable.

There are many other pressures on the way we produce our food, but I just need to highlight one more, if I may, before I move on to the possible solutions, because it is so important. It is that magical substance we have taken for granted for so long—water.

In a country like the United States a fifth of all grain production is dependent upon irrigation. For every pound of beef produced in the industrial system, it takes 2,000 gallons of water. That is a lot of water, and there is plenty of evidence that the Earth cannot keep up with the demand. The Ogallala Aquifer on the Great Plains, for instance, is being depleted by 1.3 trillion gallons faster than rainfall can replenish it. And when you consider that of all the water in the world, only 5 percent of it is fresh and a quarter of that sits in Lake Baikal in Siberia, there is not a lot left. Of the remaining 4 percent, nearly three-quarters of it is used in agriculture, but 30 percent of that water is wasted. If you set that figure against future predictions, then the picture gets even worse. By 2030 it is estimated that the world's farmers will need 45 percent more water than today. And yet already, because of irrigation, many of the world's largest rivers no longer reach the sea for part of the year—including, I am afraid, the Colorado and Rio Grande.

Forgive me for labouring these points, but the impact of all of this has already been immense. Over a billion people—one-seventh of the world's population—are hungry and another billion suffer from what is called "hidden hunger," which is the lack of essential vitamins and nutrients in their diets. And on the reverse side of the coin, let us not forget the other tragic fact—that over a billion people in the world are now considered overweight or obese. It is an increasingly insane picture. In one way or another, half the world finds itself on the wrong side of the food equation.

In a global ecosystem that is, to say the least, under stress, our apparently unbridled demands for energy, land, and water put overwhelming pressure on our food systems. I am not alone in thinking that the current model is simply not durable in the long term. It is not "keeping everything going continuously" and it is, therefore, not sustainable.

So what is a "sustainable food production" system? We should be very clear about it, or else we will end up with the same system that we have now, but dipped in "greenwash." For me, it has to be a form of agriculture that does not exceed the carrying capacity of its local ecosystem and which recognizes that the soil is the planet's most vital renewable resource. Topsoil is the corner-stone of the prosperity of nations. It acts as a buffer against drought and as a carbon sink, and it is the primary source of the health of all animals, plants, and people. If we degrade it, as we are doing, then Nature's capital will lose its innate resilience and it won't be very long before our human economic capital and economic systems also begin to lose their resilience.

Let's look for a moment at what very probably is not a genuinely sustainable form of agriculture for the long term, and by that I mean generations as yet unborn. In my own view it is surely not dependent upon the use of chemical pesticides, fungicides, and insecticides; nor, for that matter, upon artificial fertilizers and growth-promoters or genetic modification? You would have perhaps thought a genuinely sustainable agriculture system would be unlikely to create vast monocultures and to treat animals like machines by using industrial rearing systems. Nor would you expect it to drink the Earth dry, deplete the soil, clog streams with nutrient-rich runoff, and create, out of sight and out of mind, enormous dead zones in the oceans. You would also think, wouldn't you,

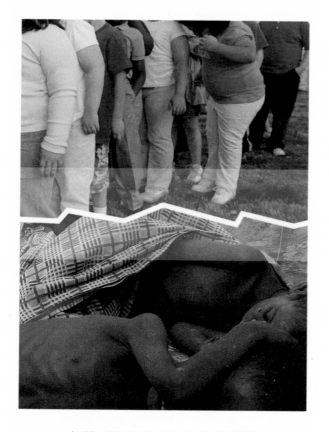

OVER A BILLION PEOPLE ARE HUNGRY
AND, ON THE REVERSE SIDE OF THE COIN, OVER
A BILLION PEOPLE IN THE WORLD ARE NOW
CONSIDERED OVERWEIGHT OR OBESE. IT IS
AN INCREASINGLY INSANE PICTURE.

that it might not lead to the destruction of whole cultures or the removal of many of the remaining small farmers around the world? Nor, presumably, would it destroy biodiversity at the same time as cultural and social diversity.

On the contrary, genuinely sustainable farming maintains the resilience of the entire ecosystem by encouraging a rich level of biodiversity in the soil, in its water supply, and in the wildlife—the birds, insects, and bees that maintain the health of the whole system. Sustainable farming also recognizes the importance to the soil of planting trees; of protecting and enhancing water-catchment systems; of mitigating, rather than adding to, climate change. To do this it must be a mixed approach: one where animal waste is recycled and organic waste is composted to build the soil's fertility. One where antibiotics are only used on animals to treat illnesses, not deployed in prophylactic doses to prevent them; and where those animals are fed on grass-based regimes as Nature intended.

Many people may think this an idealized definition—that it isn't possible in "the real world." But if you consider this the gold standard, then for food production to become more "sustainable" it has to reduce the use of those substances that are dangerous and harmful not only to human health, but also to the health of those natural systems, such as the oceans, forests, and wetlands, that provide us with the services essential to life on this planet—but which we rashly take for granted. At the same time, it has to minimize the use of nonrenewable external inputs. Fertilizers that do not come from renewable sources do not enable a sustainable approach, which ultimately comes down to giving back to Nature as much as it takes out and recognizing that there are necessary limits to what the Earth can do. Equally, it includes the need for producers to receive a reasonable price for their labors above the price of production. And that leads me to the nub of what we should consider.

Having myself tried to farm as sustainably as possible for some 26 years in England, I certainly know of plenty of current evidence that adopting an approach which mirrors the miraculous ingenuity of Nature can produce surprisingly

GENUINELY SUSTAINABLE FARMING MAINTAINS
THE RESILIENCE OF THE ENTIRE ECOSYSTEM BY
ENCOURAGING A RICH LEVEL OF BIODIVERSITY IN
THE SOIL, IN ITS WATER SUPPLY, AND IN THE WILDLIFE
THAT MAINTAIN THE HEALTH OF THE WHOLE SYSTEM.

high yields of a wide range of vegetables, arable crops, beef, lamb, and milk. And yet we are told ceaselessly that sustainable or organic agriculture cannot feed the world. I find this claim very hard to understand. Especially when you consider the findings of an impeccably well-researched International Assessment of Agricultural Knowledge, Science and Technology for Development, conducted in 2008 by the United Nations. The report drew on evidence from more than 400 scientists worldwide and concluded that small-scale, family-based farming systems, adopting so-called agro-ecological approaches, were among the most productive systems in developing countries. This was a major study and a very explicit statement. And yet, for some strange reason, the conclusions of this exhaustive report seem to have vanished without trace.

This is the heart of the problem. Why it is that an industrialized system, deeply dependent on fossil fuels and chemical treatments, is promoted as viable, while a much less damaging one is rubbished and condemned as unfit for purpose?

The reasons lie in the anomalies that exist behind the scenes.

First, we should look at the slack in the system. Under the current, inherently unsustainable system, in the developed world we actually throw away approximately 40 percent of the food we have bought. Food is now much cheaper than it was, and one of the unexpected consequences of this is, perhaps, that we do not value it as once we did. I cannot help feeling some of this problem could be avoided with better food education. You only have to consider the progress the First Lady, Mrs. Obama, has achieved by launching her "Let's Move" campaign—a wonderful initiative. Manufacturers are making their "Healthy Weight Commitment" and pledging to cut 1.5 trillion calories a year from their products; Walmart has promised to sell products with less sugar, salt, and trans fats, and to reduce their prices on healthy items like fresh fruits and vegetables; and with the First Lady's big drive to improve healthy eating in schools and the excellent thought of urging doctors to write out prescriptions for exercise—these are marvelous ideas that I am sure will make a major difference.

Alas, in developing countries approximately 40 percent of food is lost between farm and market. Could that be remedied too, by better on-farm storage? And we should also remember that many, if not most, of the farmers in the developing world are achieving a fraction of the yields they might do if the soil was nurtured more with an eye to organic matter content and improved water management.

However, the really big issue we need to consider is how conventional, agri-industrial techniques are able to achieve the success they do, and how we measure that success. And here I come to the aspect of food production that troubles me most.

The well-known commentator on food matters Michael Pollan pointed out recently that, so far, the combined market for local and organic food, both in the United States and Europe, has only reached around 2 or 3 percent of total sales. And the reason, he says, is quite simple. It is the difficulty in making sustainable farming more profitable for producers and sustainable food more affordable for consumers. With so much growing concern about this, my International Sustainability Unit carried out a study into why sustainable food production systems struggle to make a profit, and how it is that intensively produced food costs less. The answer to that last question may seem obvious, but my ISU study reveals a less apparent reason.

It looked at five case studies and discovered two things: firstly, that the system of farm subsidies is geared in such a way that it favors overwhelmingly those kinds of agricultural techniques that are responsible for the many problems I have just outlined; and secondly, that the cost of that damage is not factored into the price of food production. Consider, for example, what happens when pesticides get into the water supply. At the moment, the water has to be cleaned up at enormous cost to consumer water bills; the primary polluter is not charged. Or take the emissions from the manufacture and application of nitrogen fertilizer, which are potent greenhouse gases. They, too, are not costed at source into the equation.

WHY IT IS THAT AN INDUSTRIALIZED SYSTEM,
DEEPLY DEPENDENT ON FOSSIL FUELS AND
CHEMICAL TREATMENTS, IS PROMOTED AS VIABLE,
WHILE A MUCH LESS DAMAGING ONE IS RUBBISHED
AND CONDEMNED AS UNFIT FOR PURPOSE?

This has led to a situation where farmers are better off using intensive methods and where consumers who would prefer to buy sustainably produced food are unable to do so because of the price. There are many producers and consumers who want to do the right thing, but as things stand, "doing the right thing" is penalized. And so this raises an admittedly difficult question: Has the time arrived when a long, hard look is needed at the way public subsidies are generally geared? And should the recalibration of that gearing be considered so that it helps healthier approaches and techniques? Could there be benefits if public finance were redirected so that subsidies are linked specifically to farming practices that are more sustainable, less polluting, and of wide benefit to the public interest, rather than what many environmental experts have called the curiously "perverse" economic incentive system that too frequently directs food production?

The point, surely, is to achieve a situation where the production of healthier food is rewarded and becomes more affordable and the

Earth's capital is not so eroded. Nobody wants food prices to go up, but if it is the case that the present low price of intensively produced food in developed countries is actually an illusion, only made possible by transferring the costs of cleaning up pollution or dealing with human health problems onto other agencies, then could correcting these anomalies result in a more beneficial arena where nobody is actually worse off in net terms? It would simply be a more honest form of accounting that may make it more desirable for producers to operate more sustainably—particularly if subsidies were redirected to benefit sustainable systems of production. It is a question worth considering, and I only ask it because my concern is simply that we seek to produce the healthiest food possible from the healthiest environment possible—for the long term—and to ensure that it is affordable for ordinary consumers.

There are, after all, already precedents for these kinds of measures, particularly, for instance, in the way that governments around the world have stimulated the growth of the renewable energy market by the provision of market mechanisms and feed-in tariffs. Could what has been done for energy production be applied to food? Is this worth considering? After all, it could have a very powerful, transformative effect on the market for sustainably produced food, with benefits all around.

Certainly, the UN's Environment Program inspires hope when it estimates that the "greening" of agriculture and fisheries would increase economic value per year by 11 percent by 2050. The hugely overstretched stocks of the Northeast Atlantic bluefin tuna is a case in point, where it is estimated that a transition to sustainable fisheries management could generate a profit of more than $500 million every year, as compared to the current figure of $70 million—and that is after having received $120 million in subsidies. It is also worth bearing in mind that these sorts of policies, which encourage more diversity, in terms of landscape, community, and products, often generate all sorts of other positive results too— in tourism, forestry, and industry.

This all depends upon us deepening our

understanding of the relationship between food, energy, water, and economic security, and then creating policies which reward producers who base their farming systems on these principles. Simply because, if we do not consider the whole picture and take steps with the health of the whole system in mind, not only will we suffer from rising food prices, we will also see the overall resilience of our economies and, in some instances, our ecological and social systems too, becoming dangerously unstable.

If we do take such important steps, it seems to me that we would also have to question whether it is responsible in the long term to have most of our food coming from highly centralized processing and distribution systems. Raw materials are often sourced many thousands of miles away from where we live; meat is pro-cessed in vast factories and then transported great distances before being sold. In light of the kinds of events we have been witnessing more frequently of late, such as the horrific floods in Pakistan last year and in Australia a few months ago, it is very easy to imagine that with systems

THE FACT IS THAT FOOD PRODUCTION IS PART
OF A WIDER SOCIOECONOMIC LANDSCAPE. WE HAVE
TO RECOGNIZE THAT SOCIAL AND ECONOMIC
STABILITY IS BUILT UPON VALUING AND SUPPORTING
LOCAL COMMUNITIES AND THEIR TRADITIONS.

concentrated in such intense, large-scale ways, these events could quickly escalate into a global food crisis. We have to consider how we achieve food security in a world where commodity food prices will inevitably rise. So, could one way be to put more emphasis on re-localizing the production and distribution of key staple foods? Wouldn't that create the sort of buffer we will need if we are to face increasingly volatile and unpredictable world market prices?

The fact is that food production is part of a wider socioeconomic landscape. We have to recognize that social and economic stability is built upon valuing and supporting local communities and their traditions. Smallholder agriculture therefore has a pivotal role. Imagine if there were a global food shortage; if it became much harder to import food in today's quantities, where would countries turn to for their staple foods? Is there not more resilience in a system where the necessary staple foods are produced locally, so that if there are shocks to the system, there won't be panic? And what is more, not only can it be much more productive than it currently is, strengthening small farm production could be a major force in preserving the traditional knowledge and biodiversity that we lose at our peril.

So might it be wise, given the rather difficult situation we appear to be in, that if we do look at regearing the way subsidies work, we include policies that focus funding on strengthening economic and environmental diversity? This diversity is at the root of building resilient economies that have the adaptive capacity to deal with the increasingly severe and frequent shocks that affect us all.

I am a historian, not an economist, but what I am hinting at here is that it is surely time to grasp one of the biggest nettles of all and reassess what has become a fundamental aspect of our entire economic model. As far as I can see, responding to the problems we have with a "business as usual" approach toward the way in which we measure GDP offers us only short-term relief. It does not promise a long-term cure. Why? Because we cannot possibly maintain the approach in the long term if we continue to consume our planet as rapaciously as we are doing. Capitalism depends upon capital, but our capital ultimately depends upon the health of Nature's capital. Whether we like it or not, the two are in fact inseparable.

There are alternative ways to grow our food which, if used with new technology—things like precision irrigation, for instance—would go a very long way to resolving some of the problems we face. If they are underpinned by smarter financial ways of supporting them, they could strengthen the resilience of our agriculture, marine, and energy systems. We could ensure a means of supply that is capable of withstanding the sorts of sudden fluctuations on international markets which are bound to come our way, as the price of oil goes up and the impact of our accelerating disruption of entire natural systems becomes greater.

In essence what I am suggesting here is something very simple. We need to include in the bottom line the true costs of food production— the true financial costs and the true costs to the Earth. It is what I suppose you could call "Accounting for Sustainability," a name I gave to a project I set up in 2005, initially to encourage businesses to expand their accounting process so that it incorporates the interconnected impact of financial, environmental, and social elements on their long-term performance. What if Accounting for Sustainability were applied to the agricultural sector? This was certainly the implicit suggestion in a recent and very important study by the UN. The Economics of Ecosystems and Biodiversity, or TEEB, assessed the multitrillion-dollar importance to the world's economy of the natural world and concluded that the present system of national accounts needs to be upgraded rapidly so they include the health of natural capital, and thereby accurately reflect how the services offered by natural ecosystems are performing—let alone are paid for. Incidentally, to create a genuine market for such services—in the same way as a carbon market has been created—could conceivably make a substantial contribution to reducing poverty in the developing world.

This is very important. If we hope to redress the market failure that will otherwise blight the lives of future generations, we have to see that there is a direct relationship between the resilience of the planet's ecosystems and the resilience of our national economies.

Essentially, we have to do more today to avert the catastrophes of tomorrow and we can only do that by reframing the way we approach the economic problems that confront us. We have to put Nature back at the heart of the equation. If we are to make our agricultural and marine systems (and therefore our economies) resilient in the long term, then we have to design policies in every sector that bring the true costs of environmental destruction and the depletion of natural capital to the fore and support an ecosystem-based approach. And we have to nurture and support the communities of smallholders and family farmers.

I trust that these thoughts will help to fire debates and focus our thoughts. Who knows, perhaps we might be able to herald a new "Washington Consensus." Like the previous version which has so dominated economic thinking around the world, it could be a consensus that acknowledges the need for markets and the role of the private sector, but which also embraces the urgent need for a rounded approach—one that recognizes the real opportunities and tradeoffs needed to build a food system that enhances and ensures the maintenance of social, economic, and environmental capital.

The new food movement could be at the heart of this Consensus, acting as an agent for truly transformational change; not just by addressing the challenges of making our food systems more sustainable and secure but also because, as far as I am concerned, agriculture—not agri-industry— holds the key to the improvement of public health, the expansion of rural employment, the enrichment of education, and the enhancement of quality of life.

Critically, such a new consensus might embrace the willingness of all aspects of society—the public, private, and NGO sectors, large corporations and small organizations—to work together to build an economic model built upon resilience and diversity, which are the two great characteristics of your nation. Such a partnership is vital; indeed, it has never been needed more and I am tremendously inspired by recent initiatives in the

United States. You cannot help but feel hopeful when huge corporations like Walmart back local sourcing of food and decide to stock their shelves with sustainable or organic produce. Industry is clearly listening. Everyone has to work together, and we all have to recognize the principle that Mahatma Gandhi observed so incisively when he said that "we may utilize the gifts of Nature just as we choose, but in her books the debts are always equal to the credits."

It is, I feel, our apparent reluctance to recognize the interrelated nature of the problems and therefore the solutions that lies at the heart of our predicament and certainly on our ability to determine the future of food. How we deal with this systemic failure in our thinking will define us as a civilization and determine our survival. Let me end with the words of one of your own founding fathers and visionaries. It was George Washington who entreated your forebears to "raise a standard to which the wise and honest can repair; the rest is in the hands of God"—and, indeed, as so often in the past, in the hands of your great country, the United States of America.

THE INDUSTRIAL MODEL HAS CAUSED ENORMOUS
DAMAGE, IN A REMARKABLY BRIEF PERIOD OF TIME,
AND WE HAVE NO CHOICE BUT TO SEEK A BETTER ONE.

FOR YEARS Prince Charles has challenged the assumptions of industrial agriculture and criticized the behavior of large agribusiness firms. He's been one of the few world leaders brave enough to say–publicly, not just privately– that the current system is unsustainable. In return for that honesty the Prince has been attacked on many occasions by defenders of the status quo. Why should anyone, his accusers ask, listen to what Prince Charles has to say about agriculture? That question has a simple answer: The Prince knows what he's talking about. His criticisms of how we grow, process, and distribute food are right on the mark. And his proposals are sound. The personal attacks on Prince Charles have served to divert attention from the real issue: Our agricultural practices are causing tremendous harm.

As Americans raised in different states and different circumstances but united by a belief that change must come, we want to reform the nation's current system of food production. It is overly centralized and industrialized, overly controlled by a handful of companies, overly reliant on monocultures, pesticides, chemical fertilizers, chemical additives, genetically modified organisms, factory farms, and fossil fuels. Its low prices are an illusion. The real costs are much too high, and they are being imposed on some of the poorest and most vulnerable people in the United States.

Organic food, for example, isn't just better for the soil and the land. It's better for the human beings who work the land. There is some scientific debate about the health effects of pesticide residues, at minute levels, in food. But there's no debate about the effects of pesticide exposure upon the 1 to 2 million migrant farm workers who harvest America's fruits and vegetables by hand. For them, the need for organic food isn't an academic issue. It is literally a matter of life or death.

Pesticides are poisons. They have been carefully designed to kill insects, weeds, funguses, and rodents. But they can also kill human beings. The Environmental Protection Agency has estimated that every year, 10,000 to 20,000 farm workers suffer acute pesticide poisoning on the job—and that's a conservative estimate. Farm workers, their children, and the rural communities where they live are routinely exposed to these toxic chemicals. And what are the potential, long-term harms of the pesticides now being sprayed on our crops? Brain damage, lung damage, cancers of the breast, colon, lung, pancreas, and kidney, birth defects, sterility, and other ailments.

The wealthy will always eat well. It is the poor and working people in the United States who need a new, sustainable food system more than anyone else. They live in the most polluted neighborhoods. They are exposed to the worst chemicals on the job. They are sold the most processed, unhealthiest foods. And they can least afford the health problems that result.

Young children and people of color are being hurt the most. During the past 40 years, the obesity rate among American preschoolers has doubled. Among children aged six to eleven, it has tripled. Obesity has been linked to cancer, heart disease, and diabetes. Two-thirds of American adults are obese or overweight, and economists from Cornell and Lehigh universities have estimated that obesity is now responsible for 17 percent of the nation's annual medical costs: about $168 billion a year. African-Americans and Hispanics are more likely to be obese than non-Hispanic whites, and more likely to be poor. As upper-middle-class consumers increasingly seek out healthier foods, the fast food chains are targeting low-income, minority communities—much like the tobacco companies did, when wealthy and well-educated people began to quit smoking.

None of these problems were inevitable. And when things aren't inevitable, that means things

don't have to be the way they are. At Growing
Power, an organization based in Milwaukee,
Wisconsin, kids from the projects and the inner
city are learning how to grow their own food.
They are seeing how greenhouses can feed
urban communities without grocery stores, how
organic waste can be turned into fresh soil, how
farm-raised fish and fruits and vegetables can
replace hamburgers and fries as an all-American
meal. And as people feel more empowered in
their own communities, no matter how poor
and neglected, they become better citizens; they
see the connections between their choices and
the impact on those around them.

Access to good, healthy food shouldn't be
reserved for a privileged few. It should be a basic
right. And the changes being made at the
community level need to be translated into
changes at the state and federal level. At the
moment, the law too often favors corporate
interests over the public interest. The fast food
chains and agribusiness companies are earning
large profits, while shifting even larger costs
onto the rest of society. The game has been

rigged in favor of the powerful and well-connected, at the expense of everyone else.

The industrial model has caused enormous damage, in a remarkably brief period of time, and we have no choice but to seek a better one. We have no choice but to help those who are being sickened, impoverished, and abused. Because a food system based on poverty and exploitation will never be sustainable.

The founders of the organic movement understood that the health of people, livestock, and the land cannot be separated from one another—they're indivisible. If you want to achieve one of them, you have to work on behalf of them all. As the Prince noted, it's essential to "consider the whole picture and take steps with the whole system in mind." To do otherwise is to miss the point.

A new food system is now emerging, as more Americans see what's happening, understand the consequences—and start to take action. This new system will be much more diverse, resilient, and democratic. It will take the long view. Across the United States, communities are rejecting the industrial model of food production and creating a new one. People are shopping at farmers' markets, building school gardens, planting vegetables in their backyards. Perhaps the most important change is a new attitude toward food, a change in mindset. Instead of being passive consumers, eating the junk food marketed on TV, millions of people are educating themselves, changing what they eat and where they buy it. They are becoming empowered.

It's not too late. What's gone wrong in our food system can be reversed. A better way of doing things is still possible. The next generation can be fitter, healthier, wiser, and more compassionate than the last one. That is the basic message of the Prince's speech, and we wholeheartedly agree.

WILL ALLEN AND ERIC SCHLOSSER

REFERENCES

Brown, Lester. "The Great Food Crisis of 2011."
www.foreignpolicy.com. January 10, 2011.

Boyle, J. Patrick. "Corn Ethanol: Burning Up Food Budgets."
The Lincoln Journal Star Online (www.journalstar.com).
April 19, 2011.

The Economist. "No Easy Fix." www.economist.com.
February 24, 2011.

Food and Agriculture Organization (FAO). *Global Food Losses
and Food Waste*. Rome: FAO, 2011.

Gleick, P. H. "Making Every Drop Count." *Scientific American*
284 (February 2001): 40–45.

International Assessment of Agricultural Knowledge, Science
and Technology for Development (IAASTD). *Agriculture at
a Crossroads*. IAASTD, April 2008.

Pimentel, David. "Soil Erosion: A Food and Environmental
Threat." *Journal of Environment, Development and
Sustainability* 8 (March 2006): 119–137.

Pollan, Michael. *The Omnivore's Dilemma: The Search for a
Perfect Meal in a Fast-Food World*. London: Bloomsbury
Publishing, 2007.

The Prince's Charities' International Sustainability Unit (ISU).
*Transitioning to Sustainable and Resilient Fisheries*.
London: ISU, March 2011.

United Nations Environment Programme (UNEP). *Towards a
Green Economy: Pathways to Sustainable Development and
Poverty Eradication*. UNEP, 2011.

ACKNOWLEDGMENTS

HRH The Prince of Wales would like to express his gratitude to the following organizations and individuals whose sponsorship and support made a crucial difference in ensuring the success of the Future of Food conference, and without whose assistance, the event would not have taken place and the subsequent book would not have existed.

**Conference organizing partners:** Georgetown University; *The Washington Post;* The Sustainable Food Trust; The Prince of Wales' International Sustainability Unit (ISU).

**Research and support in the preparation of the speech:** Ian Skelly; Justin Mundy; Clive Alderton.

**Program and event coordination:** Eric Schlosser; Robert Martin; Patrick Holden; Mary Jordan; Justin Mundy; Ken Wilson; Scott Cullen; Virginia Clarke.

**Main sponsors:** Mars Inc.; Whole Foods Market; Cervena Natural Tender Venison; Hilton Worldwide.

**Thanks to:** Applegate Farms; The California Endowment; The Sustainable Agriculture & Food Systems Funders (SAFSF); Sarah Weiner, Seedling Projects; Kaiser Permanente; DC Central Kitchen; BCV Architects; Amy Barboro Design; Freshfarm Markets; US Botanic Garden; Stonyfield; Cornell Douglas Foundation; Wallace Genetic Foundation; Brown-Forman Corporation; Liz Earle.

**Special thanks to:** GRACE Communications Foundation; Bon Appétit Management Company.

**With gratitude to:** Rodale Inc., whose deep family commitment to the cause of sustainable agriculture made this book a reality, with particular thanks to Maria Rodale, CEO, and Pam Krauss, editor, who guided us along; Kelly Doe for her time and talent to design the visual look of this book and Stuart Bradford for the illustrations; Patrick Holden for his tireless efforts on behalf of a sustainable future; and Laurie David, whose idea it was to publish a book of the speech and followed it through to its conclusion.

To learn more or to get involved,
please visit OnTheFutureOfFood.org.

The Prince's Charities is a group of not-for-profit organizations of which The Prince of Wales is patron or president; 18 of the 20 charities were founded personally by The Prince.

The Prince has shown a strong personal interest in environmental issues for decades. The main themes to which he most often returns are the need for sustainable development, for responsible stewardship of our natural resources, and for global co-operation to protect our environmental heritage.

In 2004 HRH The Prince of Wales established the Accounting for Sustainability Project (A4S) "to help ensure that we are not battling to meet 21st century challenges with, at best, 20th century decision-making and reporting systems." A4S works with businesses, investors, the public sector, accounting bodies, NGOs, and academics to develop practical guidance and tools for embedding sustainability into decision-making and reporting processes. To date, the project has involved the collaboration of more than public and private sector organizations.

For more information on the Prince's Charities and the A4S Project, please visit princeofwales.gov.uk.

## OTHER WORKS BY THE AUTHOR

*Harmony: A New Way of Looking at Our World* was published in 2010 by HarperCollins and cowritten with Tony Juniper and Ian Skelly.